FILMY DASTAANS

MANISHA

ISBN 979-888546569-4

Contents

Contents

Acknowledgements

We want to thank our readers who are reading this book, our family members for supporting us,our Kashish Publication, our editor, God for helping us in this journey and special thanks to the most important ones, our co-authors, for sharing your moments that you lived.

Thanks to each and every co-author and member of our "Filmy Dastaans". We are blessed to have you in our lives. Without you, this book would not have been successfully completed and once again a big thanks to our readers for choosing this book.

Disclaimer

FILMY DASTAANS is a collection of narrative poems, prose, short stories, quotes, and many more. The compiler and the publication team have tried their best to assemble and edit the content. Every write-up in this anthology is unique and is a result of the creative imagination of co-authors.

Hence in case of any plagiarism detection, neither the compiler nor the publication house will be held responsible.

Co-authors will be individually responsible for their creations

About Us

Kashish Publications is a growing platform for all the budding writers to fulfill their dream. It is founded by Kashish Soni,a budding writer who believe that writing is the magic to heal one's heart.

"*YOU DREAM, WE ACCOMPLISHED!*"

You can contact us for solo publishing or for compiling a one of our own.

Instagram id- @kashish_publications

Gmail- sonikashish004@gmail.com

About The Compiler

Manisha, author of book 'Extrovertly Introvert, has completed her Masters degree in Development Studies from Indian Institute of Technology (IIT Mandi).

She has compiled 5 anthologies including this one – Fantasy World, Birds of a Feather, Baatein aur Yaadein, Clash of Thoughts, Filmy Dastaans.

She has also contributed in various anthologies.

One can reach her on Instagram @extrovertly__introvert.

Her blog: extrovertly--introvert.blogspot.com

Founder's Desk

1. Kashish Soni

Things 3 IDIOTS taught us-

- It is not important to be a doctor or an engineer to be successful in life. Just follow your passion and success will come to you by itself.

- We don't need a lot of friends to enjoy our school/college's life. We need only those who are loyal.

- Bad times comes in every person's life. So, we should be strong enough to overcome these times.

- At times, we are unable to decide what to do & as the result we take wrong steps like suicide. But at that time remember what Rancho(Aamir Khan) said, "Think about your parents once and then you will be unable to do such steps".

- Marks doesn't matter everytime. Sometimes knowledge can play more important role in our life than marks.

Co-author's Desk

2. Maria Johnson

Maria Johnson call her Maya. Born and bought up in Kerala. Completed post-graduation in Accounting and Finance. Currently pursuing Acca & pgdm mainly specialized in Human Resource Management . Started her writing career through an online platform named Pratilipi. First writeup was a love story - Sainayude Pranayam.

The Last Night

Later but not, the dark night sparrow
Just crawled
Have u heard of that night man
With a hammer in his arms
Bloody eyes and a masky face
In the ravishing rain
hearing his footsteps
Feel like death is near
Without a second thought he laughs
And smashes with his hammer
All i remember was blood
The red blood creating a red pool
All over me...
Later i close my eyes, Take my last breathe
Saying bye to all.

3. Noor Tabassum

The name of the author is Noor Tabassum. Writing is her passion. She has participated in more than 200 anthologies as co author and has also written solo books called Sensibles and Twisted Firsts. She is a nature lover and loves to lead a simple life. She expresses all her feelings in her writings as she thinks it is the most powerful medium to communicate. She has won many writing competitions, and her articles have been published in many magazines too. She enjoys writing poems and short stories. Her stories have been published in the Times of India newspaper too. Her Instagram id is @noortabassumali123.

Rockstar

Rockstar is one of the most romantic and efficacious movies of Imtiaz Ali. He has effectively brought out the burning desires of the youth, which is love and its complexities. He has excellently picturized how a person in love losses his senses before his darling.

In the movie, Janardhan (Randhir Kapoor) is a college-going boy who wants to be a successful singer. He dreams of touching the heights but is not effective in his singing. His friend tells him that he has no charm in singing because he has not faced any heartbreaks. That is why Janardhan starts following and proposing Heer (Nargis Fakhri). Heer is a high society, sophisticated and well-mannered girl. She is believed to be reserved and unfriendly with other students. Everybody thinks she is out of reach for them. But Heer becomes friendly with

Janardhan and shows her secret side. They secretly roam about in the dark blankets of the night, enjoying their and tasting every colour of life. She introduces Janadhan as Jordan to her friends, and there is no love sprouting in them.

After Heer gets marriage, they realize that they loved each other. Then starts the intricacies of life. Love for another male is a sin after marriage. But who can control the feelings? Jordan climbs the ladder of success with his talent, and then their love destroys the life of both lovers is portrayed very well in the movie.

Ranbir Kapoor has justified his character excellently, playing the role of a passionate lover. His desire, his feelings, and his wishes are excellently portrayed. His wild passion for his love, then his madness when he loses her, and his singing is mind-blowing. Nargis Fakhri has also played her character very well. Her innocence, mischief, dilemma regarding love, sickness, and encouragement are all worth watching. The music of the film is the center of attraction. The music of A R Rehman is mesmerizing.

Overall, this movie is excellent, covering every aspect of emotions. It wins the hearts of the young generation with the performances and music—a paisa vasool movie.

4. Pratik Salunkhe

He is a Management student. He is a person who loves to write what he experiences and feels. He writes and playes with words in hindi, marathi and english . He loves to be alone in his world but with that he handles and try to keep all his friends and relatives happy.

Shershah

Shershah is one of the most inspired movie in this pandemic and also for the youth. It's because he not only just made india proud from his bravery but also gave courage to all youngsters. In this we aslo got to know that love is all about feelings not a physical relationship. As they both were way far with eachother, then too they never gave up and married even caste was different. Here we can learn caste marriage is also possible, just the thinking of people should change.

You should be brave in any situation and should face it. You should always feel proud that you live in India . Always think what your heart says. Dont ever trust anyone . Keep a friendly nature so that people can come closer and can know you much better.

Jai Hind .

5. Kalaivani U V

She is kalaivani. And she hails from Chennai , Tamilnadu. She is girl with no idea for her future and now started her new journey of writing free anthologies which gives her happiness and way to express her emotions.

Fidaa

The movie " FIDAA " is a romentic and a strong emotions of the couple to prove their love is true and they are trying to prove the miscalculation of the heroine. This movie inspired me a lot in the way of romantic genre. The love of this flim can't be derived. The love was very pure and the way of deriving it was even more pure. The small misunderstanding may damage a relationship is very true by seeing this movie. I inspired a lot and that can't be removed from the bottom of my heart.

6. Shruthi

Shruthi started her writing career in 2018 with the publication of her first fiction Seven Vows in 2018. She has also co authored 8 anthologies so far.Prior to that she was working in a large IT firm. She was also actively analyzing shows like Ek Hasina Thi,Siya Ke Ram and Beyhadh in Indiaforums. She loves mythology,history and Indian culture and loves to weave story around that. Currently she had an active profile in wattpad as shruthiravi13

Bombay

The movie I want to talk about for this anthology is Mani Ratnam's Bombay. Though on the surface the movie appears to be an inter-religious love story as movie progresses we understand it's much beyond that. Set in the backdrop of communal riots that happened in 92-93 in the aftermath of Babri Masjid demolition it shows how religion corrupts humanity. When the children of Shekhar and Sairabanu are caught by goons and with kerosene in their hands question them whether they are hindu ya Muslim your heart breaks. You understand blind religious belief doesn't even spare children. The other poignant scene in the movie is when the children go missing in the riot. Banu cries I want my kids. You understand the pain of a mother is the same across religion and when Shekhar heaves a sigh of relief when he realizes the body in the mortuary is not that of his child you get relieved with him. You also understand the care of a father has no religion. The movie also shows every religion has bad elements,however it also has good elements. It's these elements cutting across religions that has held the secular fabric of India strong. The song by AR Rahman "Maloradu Malar" that spreads the message of humanity over religion is an icing on the top of this beautiful movie. Everytime I watch it ,it inspires me to protect humanity.

7. Srija Sadhukhan

Srija Sadhukhan is 19 years old girl studying BSc Biotechnology in Amity University Kolkata. Love to write poetry and a bookworm too.

3 idiots

One of the most amazing cinema I have ever seen. The true heart touching friendship of Rancho, Farhan and Raju.

Some real incidents of give up there life by Joy Lobo. Wanting to quit in search of some sunshine and some rain. That cinema taught everyone their life lessons. The way Rancho helped his friend to settle in their life, they way he hold their friendship. Being the topper he never had any attitude. Rancho taught to choose passion as profession. His "all izz well" everytime became the inspiration to proceed further without any fear. Being a trustworthy friend took risk, fought and at last he was the one who sat in the first row beside the professor virus. 3 idiot taught how to love someone without fear and also sacrifice for that. The way he took challenge with Chair, he won but never use to showcase that.

3 idiots is not only a cinema, it's a life lesson for all. It shows how much friends are important in life and should always have faith on friendship. How love is important as well as sacrifice. It's not at all a film for me, it's a reality from where we are too far.

8. Muralidhar Bansal

He is from Nepal. He is a businessman at present. He was inspired to write as a student seeing the environment around him. He loves writing as a hobby and he wants to be a good and rational businessman.

Lagaan

Many of us have seen many movies. But the movie that changed my life is lagaan (2001) by ashutosh gowariker with bhuwan (aamir khan) and gauri (gracy singh) as protagonists.

This movie inspired me a lot. The way bhuwan showed his passion to free his village from taxation against the englishmen. This inspired me that no matter what situation we may face, we should stand bold against the problems. If we win, it is the best and even if we lose, we gain experience.

Bhuwan then arranged players for his team. This is a true inspiration that atleast we should have faith hope and trust on person with charismatic powers.

The help from elizabeth didn't make bhuwan's love for gouri. This inspires no matter what level the mission may be, we shouldn't compromise with love.

Finally the cricket match held between the villagers and englishmen was the climax. Bhuwan gets hit even though he finishes the things and frees his village from taxation. This inspired me that life gers many wounds time and again but we shouldn't let our dreams hover over them. We can, we must and we will.

9. Sakshi

She study in Sainath College Of Education(D.EL.ED 2nd year)
She is 18 years old
She leave in Sonipat, Haryana
She did her 10 class from Vikas Bharti Public School Sector 24 Rohini
She passed out from School Of excellence sector 17
She has one Sibling in 6th standard
She has a family of 6 members
Her father name is Bhopal Singh he is a businessman
Her mother name is Seema is homemaker

Dangal

There even the storms are defeated, where the boats are stubborn.If you have faith in God, then you will get what is written in your destiny.But if you have faith in yourself, then God will write whatever you want.

Although the lines written above indicate the mantra of success, but at the same time these lines fit perfectly for Aamir Khan's movie Dangal based on the life of Mahavir Singh Phogat.In our society, girls still do not get the place which is given to boys. Trying to stop girls step by step by comparing them with boys. But this movie bypasses this thinking. He becomes an example for those fathers who love their daughters. considers them less than sons. Goal should be set in life Discipline and dedication Every parent thinks well for their children. Children are like earthen pots .Due to the discipline of Mahavir Singh

Phogat, his daughters Geeta and Babita also feel the same way. But Mahavir Singh Phogat ignores such people. He gives wrestling training to his daughters regardless of the people. Like their father, Geeta and Babita also pay attention to their wrestling training without caring for anyone. Today Geeta and Babita are an example for all the girls.

This movie inspired me a lot i get to learn lot for things from it. The main thing I learned is that we have to be determined on our aim. And once we set our goal we should not take the step back insted of it if ther is any trouble so we have to find where we are getting the problem and then find the solution for it. Even if my parents are doing hardwork for our needs and giving me support so it's my duty also to prove myself and give them the best result of there result and do something big in my life. It means if your dreams don't scare you, they are too small as success is not given it is earned. So I have to earn my success with my hard work.

10. Tejaswi Pappu

Tejaswi Pappu is born and brought up in vishakapatnam,andhrapradesh .she completed M.Tech. she is working as assistant professor in engineering college. She is a former educationist, Passionate writer, communication trainer ,Amateur of nature ,wanderlust and avid reader .she is a writer who shares her emotions and thoughts through words, which conveys message in amicable way.she has got pages
https://www.yourquote.in/trendytejaswi
https://www.facebook.com/trendytejaswi/
she loves inspiring young minds .she always feel 'writings is stress buster !'

Chak De India
Darkness rounded him with insults,
Talent frightened to roar out because the truth closed it's eyes!
Then a ray of hope came in the form of unorganized, wretchedly looked team of girls!
He became a monster for them,creating hardships to face the real game !
Tears of hatred hit his shoulders but he knew their pain will break the fear and transfer them as main!
First game was a disaster,
they were in the last ,laughed even by the selection lister!
Pride and pain hit their brain,

That was the turning point of the game which made the girls understand their master's voice and started true strain!

Win after win followed their team of discipline!

Not only won the game but also internal disturbances!

Stood as the champions making the world salute !

This movie showed that dark times are temporary, if you utilize the little ray to bring sunshine!

11. Riya Richard R. L

Riya Richard R. L is a young, burgeoning writer in English. She has adored writing since her girlhood. She has a unique style and distinct modus operandi in her writings- poems, quotes, short stories, novels, etc... She has worked as a Co-author in 380+ anthologies. She is from Kanyakumari district, Tamil Nadu.

Frozen

The great movie inspired me,
Proved that True love exists,
Elsa, the elder with Magic powers
Stayed herself away from her
Only sister Anna not to hurt her,,
She hid her love for Anna,
Anna, the younger being naive
Deceived by Henry's Fake love,
Heartbroken Anna had no way
She finally froze into a Statue,
Elsa, couldn't hide it anymore
She opened up her True love
which brought Anna Back,also
Anna got the love of her life, Kristoff
The whole movie proved that
True love Triumphs forever!

12. Kavitha

Kavitha is a Maths graduate working as a System Engineer at Tata consultancy services in Bangalore. She is from Gobichettipalayam, Tamilnadu.She is a creative thinker, a Math lover, love to read books and write poems. Belive in the words " Future is not what we planned for tomorrow, it is the work what we do today".

Nanban

My all time favourite film is Nanban(Tamil film). This film has the few incidents which correlates the incidents of my life and it is the turning point to an extent though.

I had friends who never left me in any situation. We were three as same in the movie. My friends were there with me and care's me a lot and uplifted me in my life.

Now I am an employee of an MNC company and I proudly say, for all my achievements the credits goes to my friends.

They both worry more than me when I face down step and happier than me in my success.

And the thing that changed me is the way we learn our life. Mugging up all the theories will not pay us anything other than struggles.

As we are humans and we have to gain knowledge from practice or doing it, thinking practically. Don't learn something that others are learning, you cannot excel in that stream for sure. Do what you mind says.

Follow your interest or passion, it will drive you the height which you doesn't imagine.

13. Rachana Saha

Rachana Saha, a budding writer. She has a great interest and love in writing. She bleeds her feelings in her diary. She is in class 8 reading in St. Xavier's Institution. She is born and brought up in Kolkata. She is co-author of many anthologies and wants to write more. She is compiler of two books THE BLANK PAGE and BLEEDING METAPHOR. Other than writings, she has a great interest in drawing.

Shershah

'Hello!'

'Hi! Kya kar rhe ho? Kal kab aoge?'

'Main kal nhi aa paunga.'

'Kyu? But you promised me na'

'Haan, mujhe yaad hain. Par mujhe Desh ke liye yaha par rehna parega'

'Par..'

'Listen! Listen. Before you say anything, main 15 din baad aunga right? Haina?

'Hmm'

'Tab mein 10 din ke liye aunga.'

'Tum bar bar aisa hi bolte hon, lekin do din baad chale jate hon'

'But believe me, iss par pakka aunga'

'Hmm. Khana kya khaogi?'

'Kuch nhi. Mann nhi hain mera. Baad mein kha lungi'

'Arrey arrey arrey! Baad mein kyu? Tum nhi khaogi to main bhi nhi khaunga'

'Tch. Itna drama? Uff.'

'Tumhare pyaar mein'

'Hm. Hm. Thikhain. Samjhti hun sab'

'Pta hain. Isliye to pyaar kiya hain tumse. Acha thik hain khub khalo ab'

'Hm. Tum bhi khalo. Dhyaan rakhna apna aur jaldi ghaar wapas ana. I miss you'

'I miss you too. Ek aur baat'

'Haan bolo na!'

'Is 15 din main call ya choti nhi likh sakhti. Main tumhe zarur chitti likhar bhejungi agar mujhe kuch ho gya to.'

'Kyu bolte ho aisa? Tumhe tu kuch idea nhi hain mera yaha kya ho rha hain'

'Mujhe pta hain. Isliye to wada nhi kar pa rhi hun ki 10 din rhungi bhi ki ya nhi; lekin aunga zarur. Chalo thik hain, main rakhti hun'

He hangs up the call.

There, he bleeds in blood and she bleeds in tears, here. Their last one hour talk was killing her. She was thinking of him as days passes by. And then, after 9 days, someone knocked at her door and gives her, his soldier's uniform and a letter as promised.

Oye Dimple,

Ha pta hain adha promise pura huya hain; 10 din na shi, 10 minute ke liye hi. Tujhe gussa aa rha hain, dukh ho rha hain, tu mujhe kale se Las mar ro rhi hain aur bitte palo ko phirse utha rhi hain.

Main teri anshu poch nhi sakti lekin sirf bol rhi hun 'Humare yaad aur humara pyaar kafi hain humare kahani ko pura karne ke liye'. Hum fauj marte bhi hain to hum e amar bola jata hain.

Ab mera hath pakar kar to nhi, yaado ko lekar apna rasta bna. Kasam humare pyaar ka, tu chunegi nyi mor, nyi kahani. Humare kahani ko kya, wo to humare pyaar hi kafi. Kabhi bhi feelings hide mat kar ke rakhna. Ajj mein nhi bolungi ki "tu ro mat"; ajj royegi to kal hasegi na. Apne se rang kabhi bhi dur mat rakhna. Jaise hasti thi, phirse muskurana. Aur khatam karti hun yaha humare sath. Nhi karungi main tujhe aur thoda sa tang. I love you mere Janeman.

Tera adha pyaar,

Vikram

14. Anusmita Sahoo

Her name is Anusmita Sahoo. An ambitious writer ,dreamer of big achievements and believer of life full of values who loves to keep the inner voice alive and pen emotions by poems and stories captivated from life. So here she is sharing her poems with you and expecting your love and feedbacks for future endeavors.

Mary Kom

Na meri koi pehchan hai
Na jana hai kisko maine yahan
Yahan har gali mere khilaaf hai
Yaha har pal mere liye shraap hai
Mujhe udna hai bahut dur tak
Mujhe karna hai mere dil ki
Yeh logon ka kehna sunna mera kaam nahin
Darr kar jiyun aisa mera khwaab nahi
Jo mere andar jal raha hai
Wo chingari mere jeet ki hai
Jo mere vajood ko joda rha ahi
Wo koi musafir nahin mera jazba hai
Koshish karna dharm hai mera
Fir afsos ka haath thaam kar aage jana hai
Ab aayi hoon mehnat se to jeet kar jana hai
Bas thori aur lagan se mujhe meri mazil ko pana hai

15. Shubhanjali Nishad

Name of Co Author is shubhanjali nishad she hailing from kanpur up. her passion is writing. ND her hobbies is reading books ND travelling her aim is to achieve success in short time. She want to become a professional writer in his life.she completed 200+ anthology books as a co author contact with her through Gmail I'd nishadrock96@gmail.com
Instagram I'd kanha_ki_laado

Movies

Yuuuu toh khne ko filme enertainment ka jariya hoti hai par kayi filme esi hoti hai jo hme prerna de jati hai Wese toh filme dekhne mein kuch khas dilchasp nahi tha hmko pr kuch filme hai jo dil ko mere bhot bha jati hai
Esi hi kuch filmo k kya naam btau mai apko jinko jitna bhi dekhlo kbhi jeee ni bhrta
Chak de India or three idiots jese filme hme bhot kuch sikha jati hai
Hr insan pdayi mein hi awwal ni ho skta kayi esi fields hoti h jo bachho k dil ko jada bhaa jati hai
Kyuki ki rati hui chize ek umr tak he yaad reh jati h
Pr soch smjh k dil se yaad ki hui chize hmesha jeevan mein kaam ati hain pdhna likhna jaruri hai pr us hadd tk jb ap padhayi ko mn se pdho or karo kyuki ajkl bachhe sirf pesa kamana chahte hai
Paisa kmane k toh kayi jariye hote hai agar kamana hai mn se pd kr naam kmao jo fields tumhe psnd ho wo chuno unn raat bhr depression

mein jaa jaa kr raat bhr pdh kr jaan mt gvaao tum
Filmo ko tum sirf ussi najriye se
dekho jaha tm kuch seekh pao tm

16. Vijayamalathi Mani

Vijayamalathi Mani completed her Bachelor degree in English literature. She engrossed inking quotes and poetry. She is a pluviophile.Glance her musings on YQ @Violet vibes?.She wrote more than 3000 quotes on YQ. She currently compiling a anthology captioned "Miene Instinkate".She is the core member of Solaced pentacles, World of Logophiles, Inner Souls. She co-authored in 100+ anthologies.She believes via writings can win others heart.See her thoughts on Instagram @a_ariharasudhan.

Love Today

The film "Love Today",
I think something be into that,
The film show about the love,
With extreme feelings,
The hero loves heroin at first sight,
But she doesn't accept his love,
The heroin's father suspects the heroin have a love affair with hero,
And force her to leave the town,
In between that the heroin's father physically abuse the hero,
The hero leave the town and went search for the heroin,
In between that the hero's father passed away,
Hero's friends try to reveal hero's father death,
But they failed,
One of the hero's friends ends up the cremation,

After all over hero arrives his home and he broke,
The heroin come reveal her love to the hero,
But the hero denied her love,
Because " he lost everything for love",
So he denied her love!
"Love is not God"!

17. Muskan Kesarwani

Muskan Kesarwani resident of Katghar Prayagraj, she is a writer as well as a teacher and she is also fond of photography, she has written a lot of amthology so far and is publishing her book, she has got many certificates in writing and photography

Baghban

I have seen many picture stories in my whole life, I cannot name any one but I want to share with you some of those moments which inspire me to move forward, although our life is like some mysterious stories. It is not less than a movie, every day we keep getting new steps, which we have to overcome with our understanding There is a lot of unity in the family, after a few days, the children grow up, get married and start becoming their own household, the family starts breaking up, everyone starts separating only then the mother. The division of the father started, when the youngest heir of that house talked about leaving the house, everyone was surprised and asked him, son, who taught you this, the child answered thoughtfully, how good the house used to be, but now So everyone is busy in himself, the father explained that son, we do not have the same time, with time we have to leave and adopt many things, only then the child replied with great innocence, then will I grow up so busy that I too will not get your time, father replied yes son, everyone gets busy, you will be too, the son said with great gullibility, otherwise I should not grow up and should not be busy because I will grow up too Leaving both of you at home, you will cry if you guys cry, then I too will like you. I will be jealous by speaking elders and will leave Vardhya Ashram. Tears started raining from everyone's eyes, such a small child understood the difference of the whole house, but the elders of the house do not know why the elders do not understand their own parents.

18. Gaurav Trivedi

He is Gaurav Trivedi from Kanpur, a Post Graduate in Computer Applications and also a Law Batchelor, Currently He is working in Indian Railways He love to make new friends n most of his time spends among the friends.

I'm a Girl

It's not an easy thing to be me,
I'm a girl and I'm not in we,
They call me a bird I'm still not free,
The one being who's searching for liberty,
I can see the derides in their eyes,
I can feel the hindrance in their voice,
For some days you see goddess in me,
But at next just a thing of adultery,
It's not an easy thing to be me,
I'm a girl I'm not in we..

19. Manoj Jain

He is from Firozabad near Agra UP.
Having frankly nature and like to write about love and broken heart

Zindagi Na Milegi Dobara

Dilon mein tum apni betabiyan leke chal rahe ho.
Toh zinda ho tum!
Nazar mein khwaabon ki bijliyan leke chal rahe ho
Toh zinda ho tum!
Hawa ke jhonkon ke jaise aazad rehna seekho
Tum ek dariya ke jaise, leharon mein behna seekho
Har ek lamhe se tum milo khole apni baahein
Har ek pal ek naya samaa dekhe ye nigaahen,
Jo apni aankhon mein hairaniyan leke chal rahe ho
Toh zinda ho tum!
Dilon mein tum apni betabiyan leke chal rahe ho
Toh zinda ho tum!

20. Tanisha Sethi

Her name's Tanisha Sethi and is from Gurugram. She is presently in class 10th. Writing is something that gives her comfort and helps her relax. Over the past few months, she has started living this dream, and it gives her so much joy. Her parents have always supported her dreams. In her pre-childhood, she used to watch animated stories, and this has a long-lasting effect on her. Learning new things is one thing which she always enjoys. Her hobbies are Video Editing, Writing, Drawing, and painting.

Captain Fantastic

Movies, I cannot imagine my life without it. I am a big movie-fan. For me it's a way to really relax, to lose myself in a story and forget about time and place. When watching so many movies for so many years and seeing my own work I can honestly say I get most of my inspiration from movies (99% of the time without even knowing it). It also illustrates my hang towards romance and bonds between people. It gets harder and harder to find movies that really hit me like lightning. But it does happen and sometimes for the most unexpected reasons. I am very sensitive for composition, colors and overall vibe.

Captain Fantastic

One of the reasons why this movie left me speechless was because I went there without seeing any trailer, poster or even a plotline. I had no idea what this movie was about. But I was so emotional from the very first scene, wow! It's what my dreams are made of. Or not?

This movie hit me HARD. It stayed with me for days. It got me overthinking my life, this world, nature and how we treat it (even more than usual which is already a lot). It's beautiful, serious, breathtaking and funny at the same time. I don't want to tell too much about it so if you haven't seen it yet: don't read the story just dive in there!

21. T.S.Samicshaa

T.S.Samicshaa, a 17 year old teen wants to give her the best in everything she tries. She lives in the world of dreams and loves to fantasize the best of the world. She is a keen straight A student pursuing PCB with psychology having great interest in psychology and genetics. She loves to sing and is a traditional kathak dancer. She is a great elocutionist and painting and writing are her passion. She is a social bee who can mingle with anyone anywhere no matter the circumstance and loves to interact more with people abroad cause she likes to learn more about their cultures.

Yeh Jawani Hai Deewani

Apni khudgarzi ko tk
Dost seh jaate hain
Saalo ka safar
Yu tay kr jaate h
Na koi sawaal
Na koi shak
Bas meelo saath chalte h
Chahe kitne baras kyu na
Bichre ho
Ek waqt pr saab mil hi jaate h
Chahe zindagi mein
kitna bhi junoon ho
Dosto ke bagair sab

Soona soona hota h
Zindagi jeena sikhate h dost
Har mushkil se ladna sikhate h dost
Har raaz ko chupate h dost
Aur waqt aane pr usi se
Mazak udate h dost!
Pyaar aur dosti m alag sa nasha
Hota h
Pr bunny ko to sirf trekking ka nasha!
Naina ne kabhi intezaar to kiya nhi
Par har pal use yaad aate rhe wo din
Jo guzaare the bunny ke saath!

22. Sangeeta Sahu

This is Sangeeta Sahu. Sangeeta Sahu is a writer.she is a collage student of bsc 2 year .she live at village Paneka in kabirdham chhattisgarh.her hobbies are writing poetry shayaris and etc.follow me on my insta handle sangeeta_sahu20.

Miss India

Meri life ki inspiration movie "MISS INDIA " hai .ye vo movie hai jisne mujhe badal di mere think ko change kar di.ye movie me miss kirti Suresh mam main character hai .is movie me ak girl ke life me btaya Gya hai ise jab mai Dekhi thi to lga jaise ye meri story ho ...meri bhi halat unke jaisi hi family ka koi support ñhi ...jo kam mujhe pasand hai ya jo mai bnna chahti hu vo mere parents ko pasand nhi.usme ak ladki ke samne kya kya problem aati hai jaise ki uske sabse pyare dost unke dadaji unke life se chale gye fir unhone apna ghar chhod diya fir ak nayi sahar nye dost ...par ghar me support ñhi .vo apne goal ko pura krne ke liye duniya to aam bat hai vo apne family se ladh gyi jaise mai bhi ladhti hu aur vo apna goal pura krne ke liye ghar bhi chhod di ..vo bolti hai ki kbhi kisi ke liye apna career apna dream na chhode...ye jo movie hai mere liye bhut khas hai ye south ki movie hai jo bhi padh rhe honge ak bar ye movie jarur dekhe ..kyuki isne mera mind set ke sath mera attitude bhi change kiya hai.

23. Mushaab Sheikh

Mushaab Sheikh is an aspiring writer hailing from Kerala, he is a sports enthusiast and loves exploring the world through social media platforms. He is an autophile and believes in the power of words & pen!

M. S. Dhoni

The movie " MS DHONI THE UNTOLD STORY " has inspired a lot of youths to believe in themself and a lot of cricket aspirants who are demotivated due to the pandemic. His story from being a ticket collector to being one of the most successful captains the game has ever produced is something next to unimaginable. His story on how he became a cricket player, his story on how he and sakshi got married, and his struggle is truely inspiring. In that movie, Mr. Sushant singh rajput acted brilliantly and it made us believe in the quote " NEVER GIVE UP " and a lot more which can't be displayed here as the list goes very long. Without a second thought there's no better wicket keeper than him and probably he doesn't even have a competitive wicket keeper. This movie is one source of motivation every cricket aspirant needs.

24. Mohammed Niyaz

Mohammed Niyaz hails from Mumbai - The City Of Dreams. He often loves to write poetries and short music video stories for his own youtube channel. Apart from this Mohammed is currently working on his upcoming anthologies, as well writing poetries since 2013. You can find him on facebook/mohammed niyaz as well on instagram @niyazsks.

Baghban

With hands left on to the pocket less drafts.
He himself was now on a new beginning of his own craft.
Having being surrounded by his four youthful sons.
He dreamt of having a life fulfilled with peaceful tons.
As time took trials by testimonial phase.
When he was rested by his own boundaries of genes face.
He faced many ordinary events with extra ordinary lessons.
When each and every single penny worth him through sessions.
His timely charity and a helping hand made him stable.
To continue the journey of being stubborn able.
An underestimated person, whose real life story went viral.
In the awful takes of blissful revival.
Words and feelings, made his emotions printed in alphabetical copies.
Happiness relied until and top of trophies.
His name entitled the cases of numerous same.

Through pieces which he formed earned him "the reign of successful fame".

25. Adlin Thaneeba T. T.

Adlin Thaneeba T. T. is a poet and a short story writer from Kanniyakumari district. She has completed her Master of Philosophy in English from Nesamony Memorial Christian College, Marthandam. She loves to share the unforgettable incidents that happens in her life. Her world of happiness is her husband, two kids and her parents.

Something Something Unakkum Enakkum

In the movie ' Something Something Unakkum Enakkum', the hero Jeyam Ravi is in love with the heroine Trisha. He is from a well-settled rich family whereas the heroine is from a poor farmer family. They met in a marriage function of her friend who is his relative and loved each other. But his family highly opposed their love and used abusive words against her.

She had a brother, who is a farmer. He too came to the marriage function. When he came to know about his sister's love and their hatred towards her, he took her back to village.

The hero came to the village and asked her brother to allow him to marry her sister. But her brother told him that he is going to test him. As he was from a rich family, he had to work in a farm and had to get more grains than him. If he won this task, he will win the hands of her sister.

He boldly accepted to do the task and worked hard to get the hands of his lady love. Finally, his hardwork and true love won and he married

her.
This movie inspired me and I too struggled to marry a guy who is from a middle class family. My hubby's family refused to accept me. Because of our true love, we married. Now we are leading a happy life with the blessings of the God.

26. Poetry Khakholia Mundra

She is Poetry Khakholia Mundra, aged 42 years, married having two children, living in the land of Goddess Kamakhya, Guwahati Assam. She is an Mcom, Med and LLB, honours in management was lecturer in the university for sometimes. But is keen on writing her thoughts and feelings..Also she is a tea and music lover whose only abode is peace and peace.
Her motto in life is to
Live and let live
Love and let love.

Life Partner
That one movie that is
forever green in my memory and that touched my heart, my life and soul is life partner starring Govinda and other stars..
like fardeen Khan, Genelia, Tushar kapoor,
Prachi Desai, etc etc
This movie is the reality of married life and of married couples, their ups and downs after marriage be it arranged or love, life turn upside down after marriage, for marriage is not a bed of roses and if we don't realise this reality to shoulder the responsibility befalling marriage, it harshly turmoils the couples and their marriage resulting in divorce and separation.
Patience, perseverence

faith and understanding are the keynotes of a married life, which touched and motivated me in my marriage to apply all of it to add both spice and rice in marriage...

And most touching was the dialogue that out of the three couples one says who did love marriage, whose life was very happenning and blissful when lovers but things changed after marriage.

The lover now turned hhusband fardeen Khan says to his girlfriend Genelia now wife, that Sanjana tum kab badi hogi ab bhi agar tum girlfriend hi bani rahogi to hamare rishte se badbu aane lagegi...

Its high time u stop behaving like a girlfriend and start sharing home responsibility as wife..

This is so true for we girls who become women soon after marriage, and whole lot expectations fall flat on our shoulders, both should balance and harmonize

so as to have a happy and a peaceful married life..!!

27. Manjeet Singh

His name is Manjeet Singh, his major works are known by his pen name Mr. Reality. He was born in Ranchi Jharkhand. He did his secondary schooling at Guru Nanak Higher Secondary School, Ranchi. And his senior secondary from St. John's Inter College Ranchi. Currently, he is pursuing a BA. English Hons (Last year) from Sarala Birla University Ranchi. His work's insights are usually based on the reality of life, which easily reflects feelings of catharsis towards readers. His creations generally exist as simplistic in nature which will definitely help you to perceive the objective behind the work.

Lakshya

I was too before like an unaware and inactive child,
Doesn't carry a moto or objective of being alive, like a freezed mind,
But suddenly got a chance to learn,
From a movie Lakshya, really got it my earn,
This story not only makes me energetic from that tragic rife,
But instantly got a taste and value of being hardwork in the life,
That's why this movie makeup my life whole change,
Instantly got up a track and the needful range,
It showed nothing matters about the past,
You'll definitely reach your destination, not matter how it vast.
Just need a heart and an empty mind,
It will bring you the need and will always remind.

Lastly got my answer anyone can be in this race and persue their goals

,

Definitely one day will cope-up the outcome and beauty of being in this Lakshya role.

Then you'll too definitely realize and know, how a movie can change your life turn!!!

Not only for Ritik Roshan but the taste of success is for every Karan.

The End

Printed by Libri Plureos GmbH in Hamburg,
Germany